The Artistry of
Bill Evans

Volume 2

2   *Autumn Leaves (Milestone M-47034)*

16   *Here's That Rainy Day (Verve 833-801-2)*

25   *I Should Care (Verve UMV-2053)*

36   *Make Someone Happy (Verve UMV-2053)*

47   *Spring Is Here (Milestone M-47034)*

54   *The Touch Of Your Lips (Fantasy 9542)*

72   *What Is This Thing Called Love? (Milestone M-47034)*

84   *What Kind Of Fool Am I? (Fantasy 9542)*

Many thanks to Warner Bros. Publications for their continuing commitment to the artistry of my late husband, Bill Evans.

Nenette Evans

c/o TRO
11 West 19th Street
New York, NY 1011

© 1995 WARNER BROS. PUBLICATIONS INC.
All Rights Reserved

Editors: David C. Olsen & Tom Roed
Cover Photo: Fantasy Records
Transcriptions by Bob Hinz

AUTUMN LEAVES

English lyric by JOHNNY MERCER
French lyric by JACQUES PREVERT

Music by JOSEPH KOSMA

Fast swing

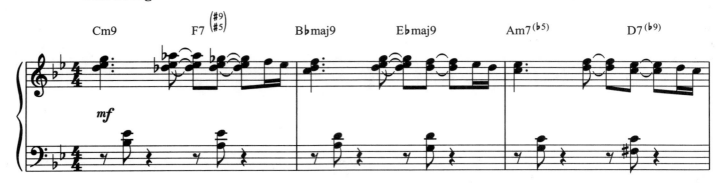

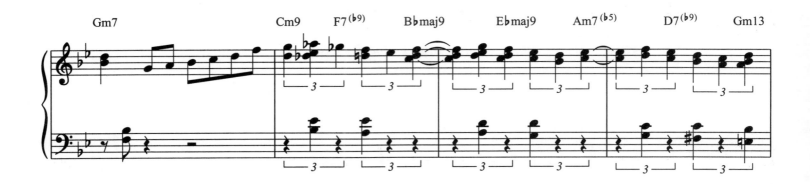

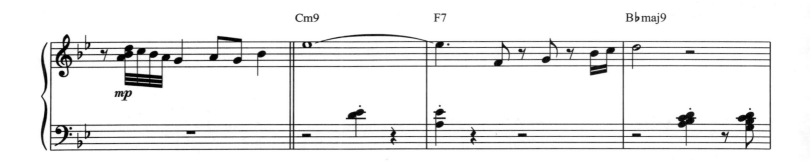

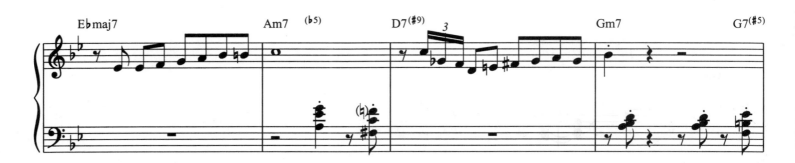

Autumn Leaves – 14 – 1

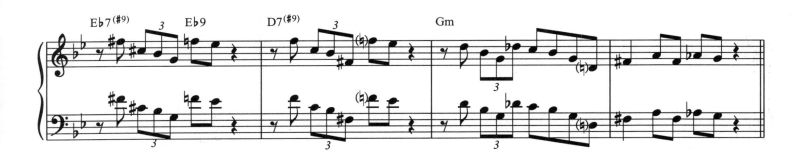

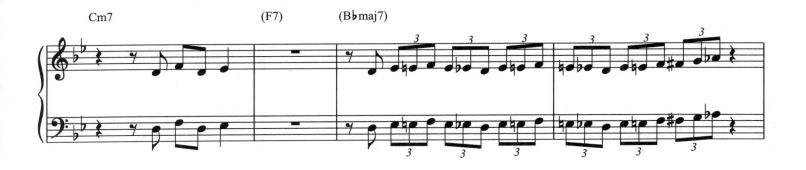

6

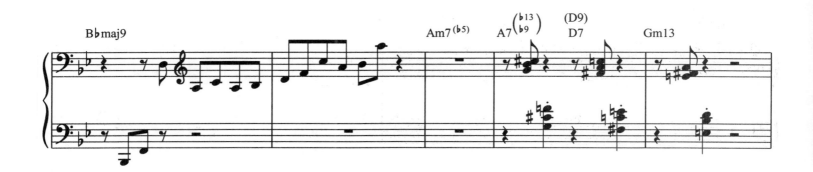

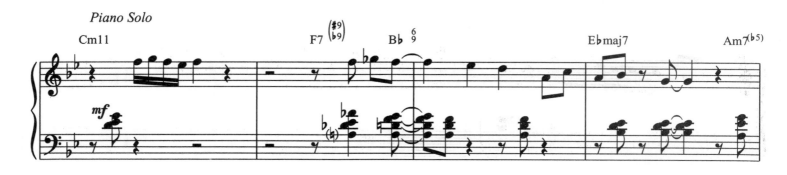

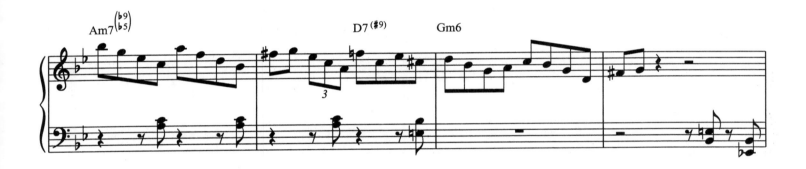

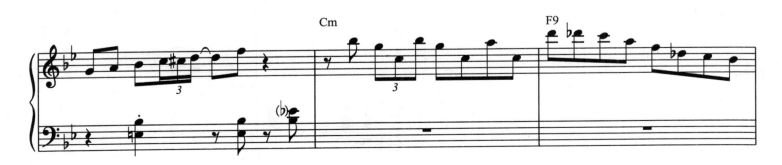

8

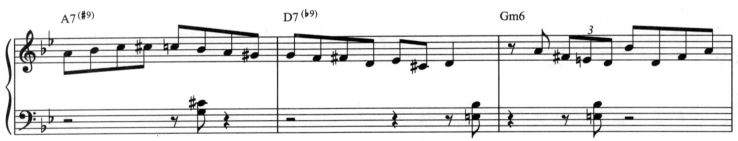

10

Autumn Leaves – 14 – 9

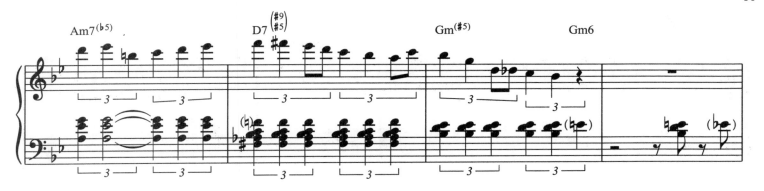

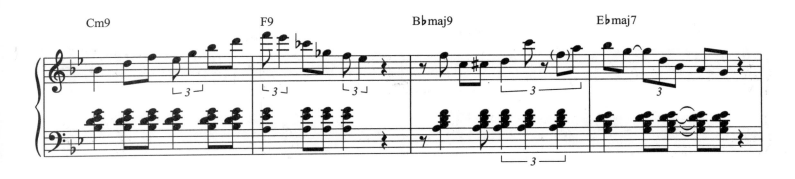

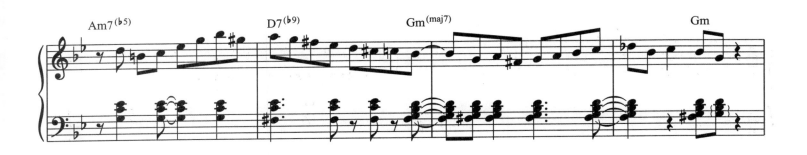

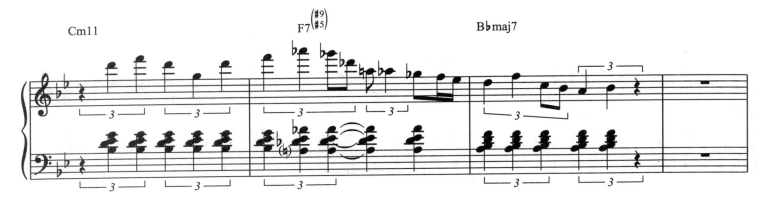

12

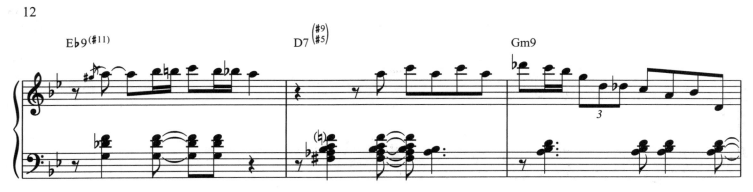

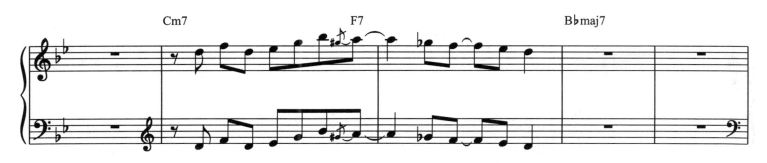

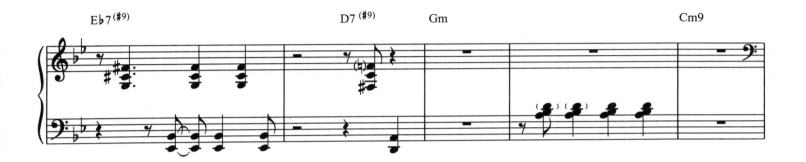

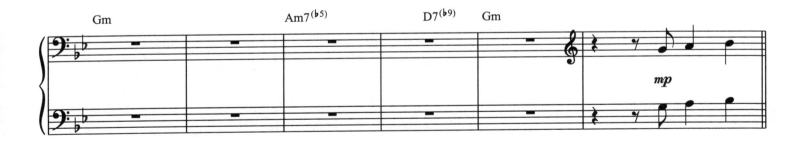

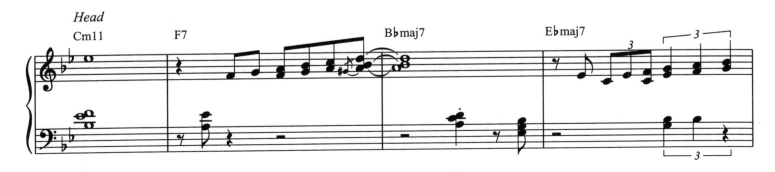

Autumn Leaves – 14 – 12

14

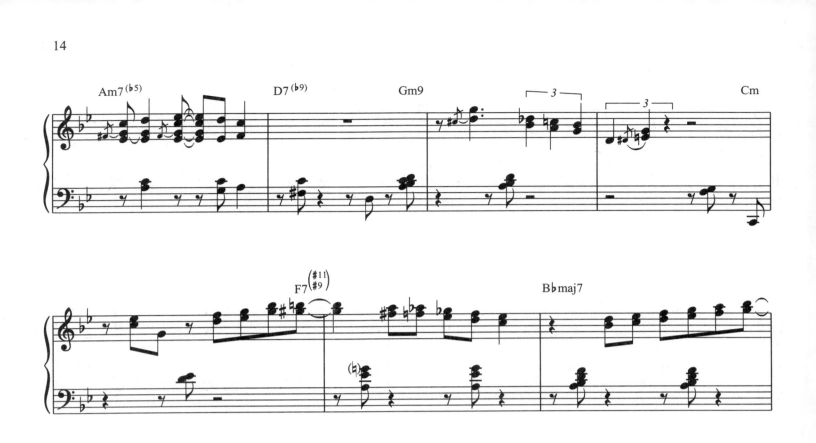

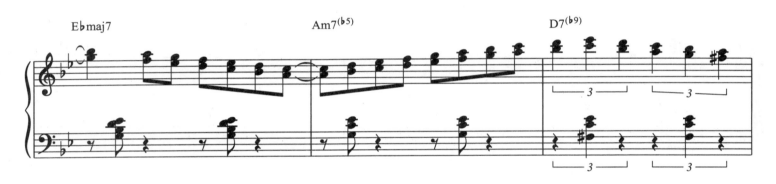

HERE'S THAT RAINY DAY

Music by JAMES VAN HEUSEN

Slowly, rubato

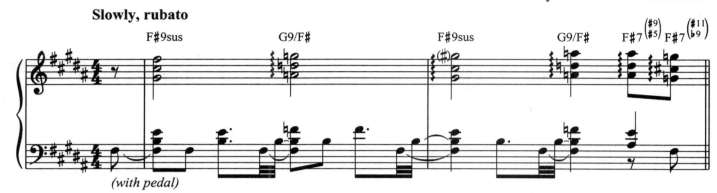

(with pedal)

Slow swing

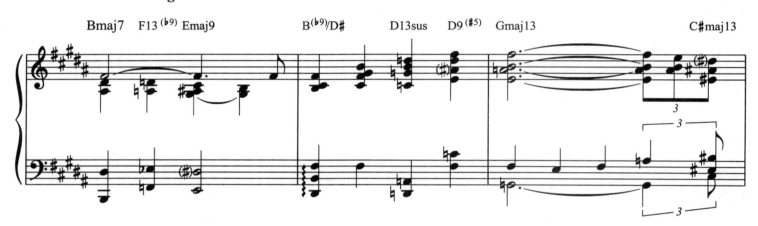

Here's That Rainy Day – 9 – 1

Here's That Rainy Day – 9 – 2

20

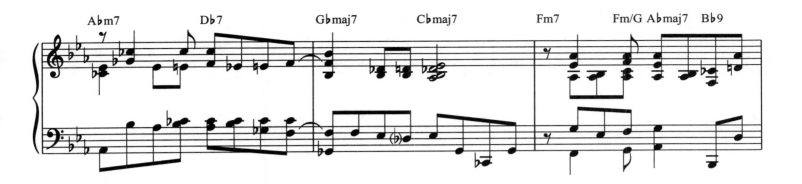

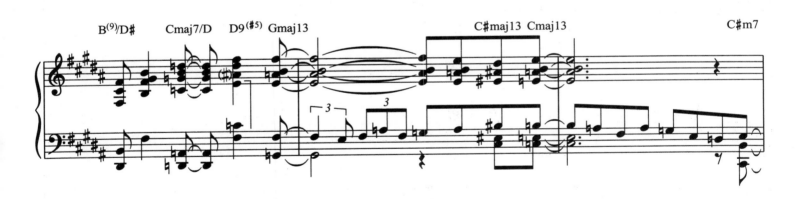

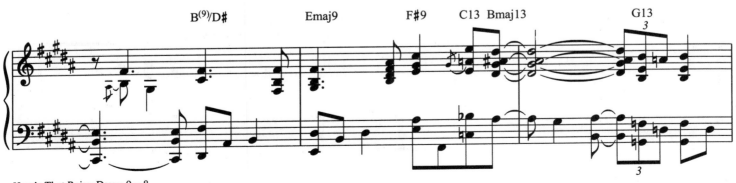

Here's That Rainy Day – 9 – 8

24

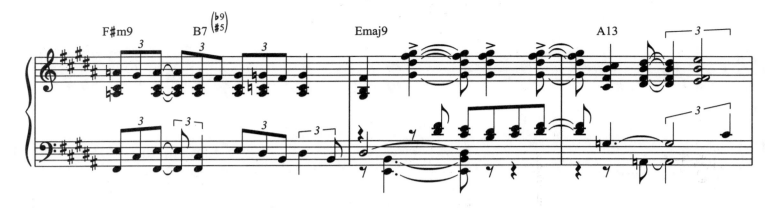

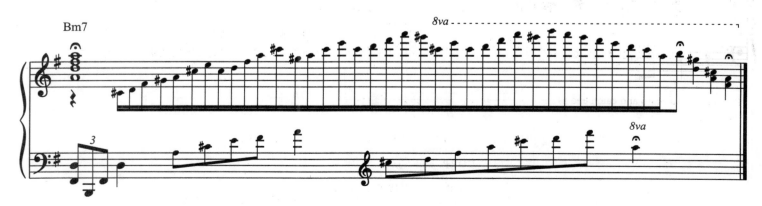

Here's That Rainy Day – 9 – 9

I SHOULD CARE

By SAMMY CAHN, AXEL STORDAHL
and PAUL WESTON

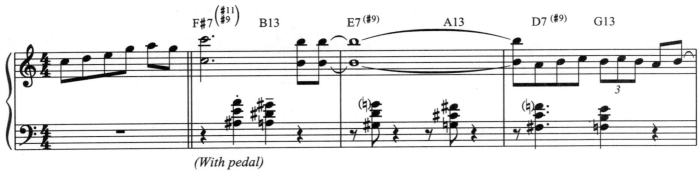

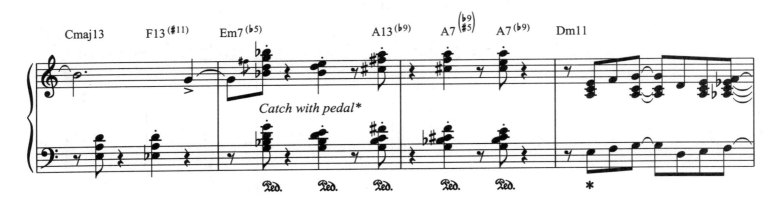

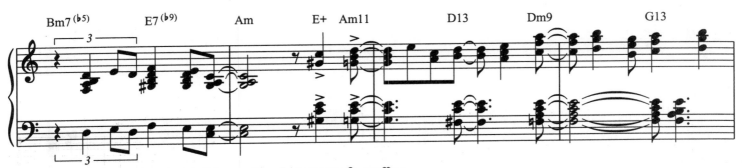

*Play chords staccato and catch end of decay with pedal to create *sfz* - *p* effect

I Should care – 11 – 1

I Should care – 11 – 3

28

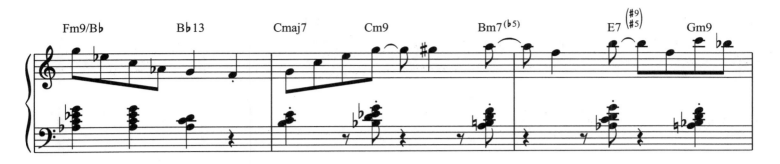
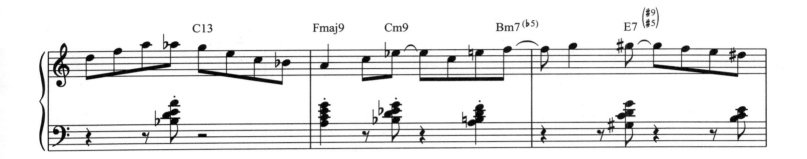

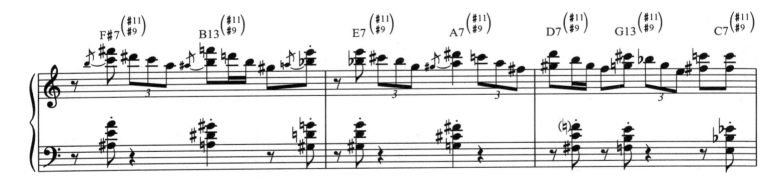

30

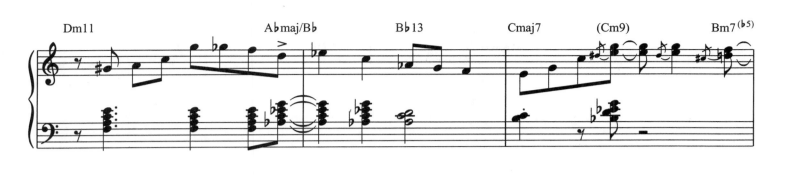

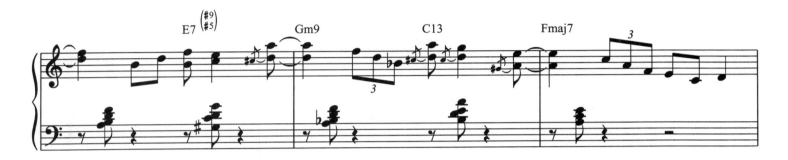

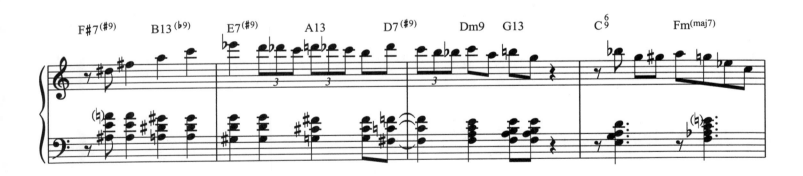

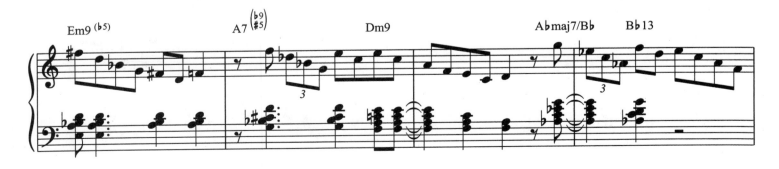

I Should care – 11 – 7

32

I Should care – 11 – 11

From DO RE MI

MAKE SOMEONE HAPPY

Words by BETTY COMDEN and ADOLPH GREEN

Music by JULE STYNE

Slowly & freely

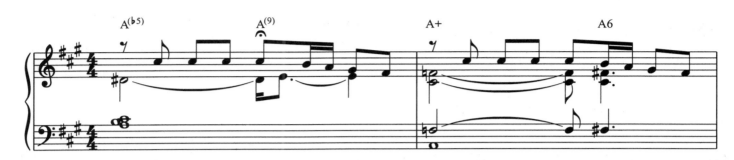

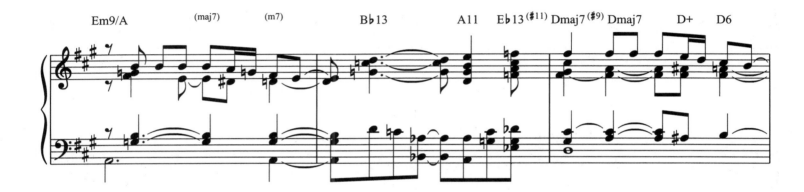

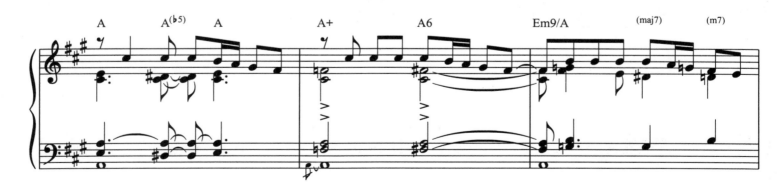

Make Someone Happy – 11 – 1

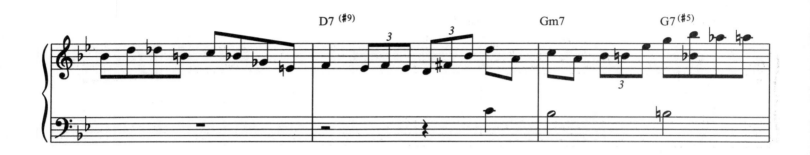

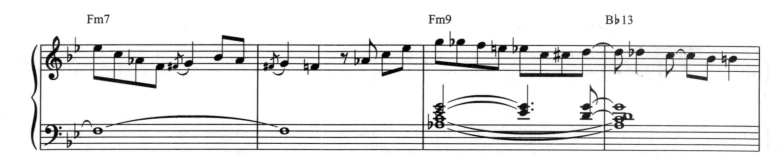

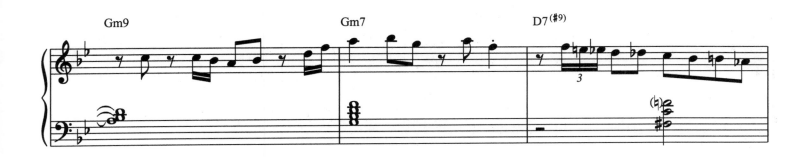

Make Someone Happy – 11 – 4

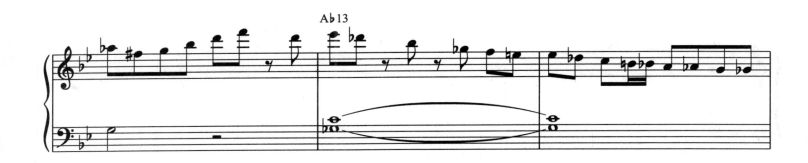

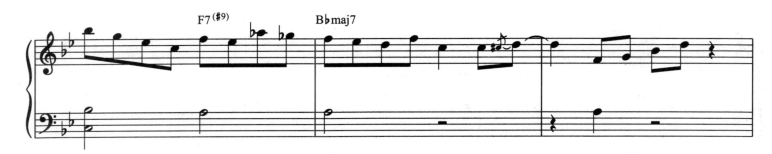

Make Someone Happy – 11 – 6

44

Slower

SPRING IS HERE

Music by RICHARD RODGERS

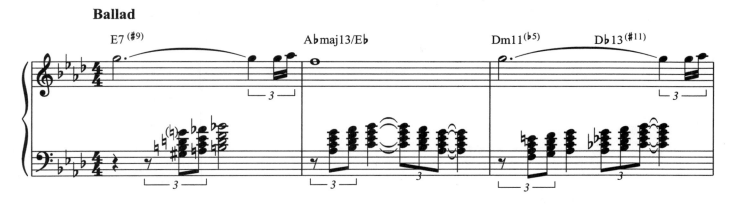

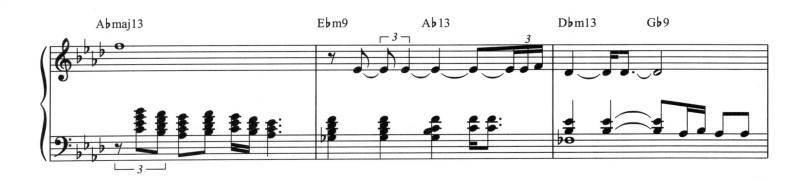

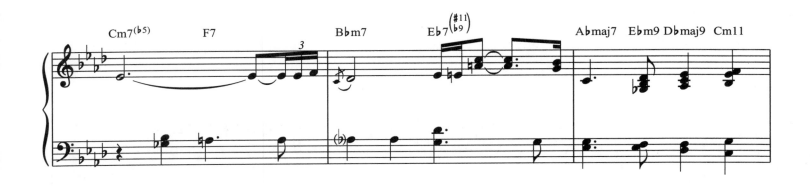

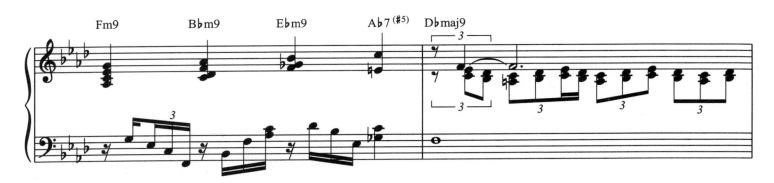

Spring Is Here – 7 – 1

50

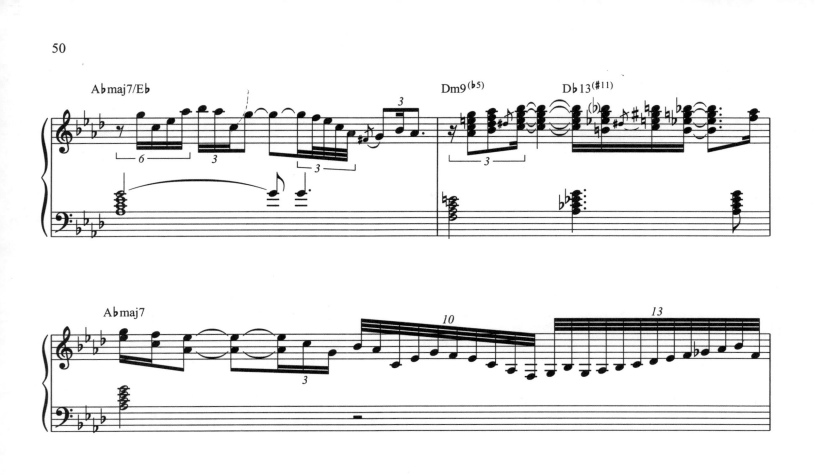

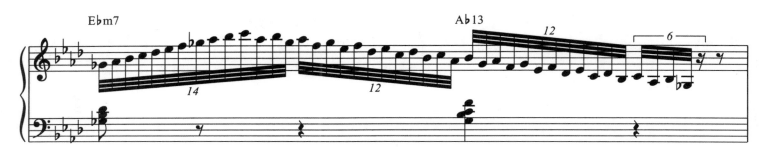

Spring Is Here – 7 – 4

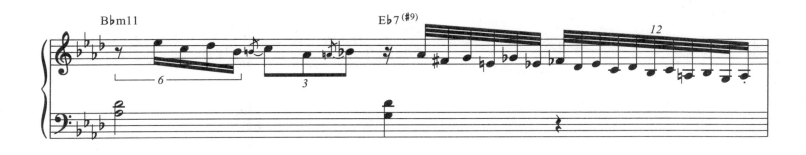

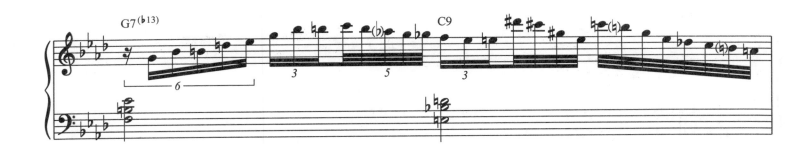

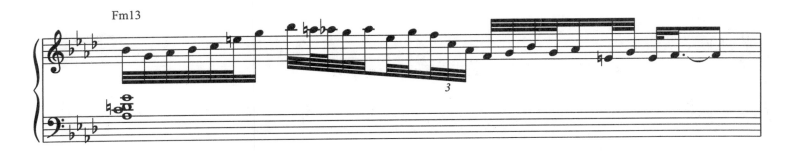

Spring Is Here – 7 – 5

52

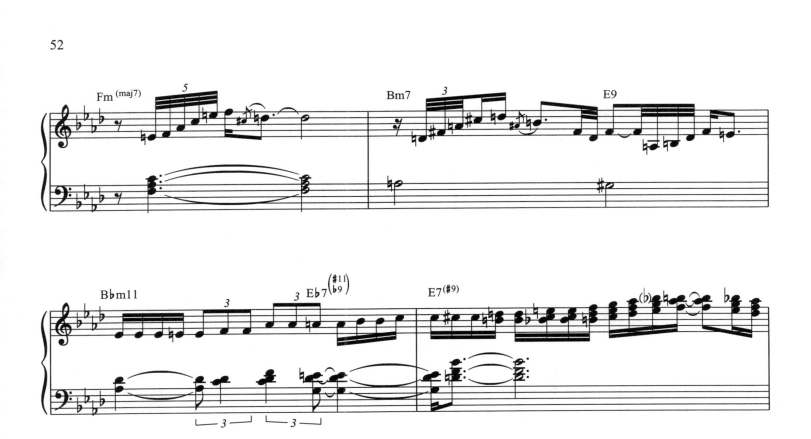

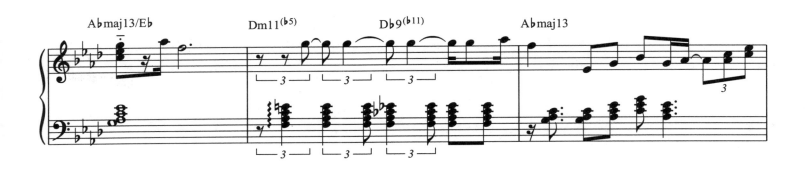

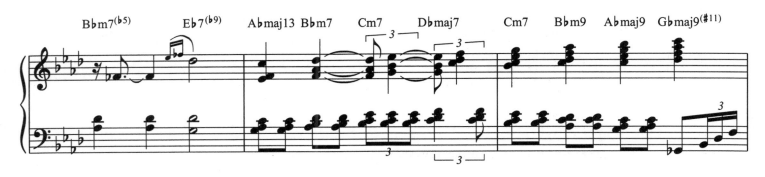

Spring Is Here – 7 – 6

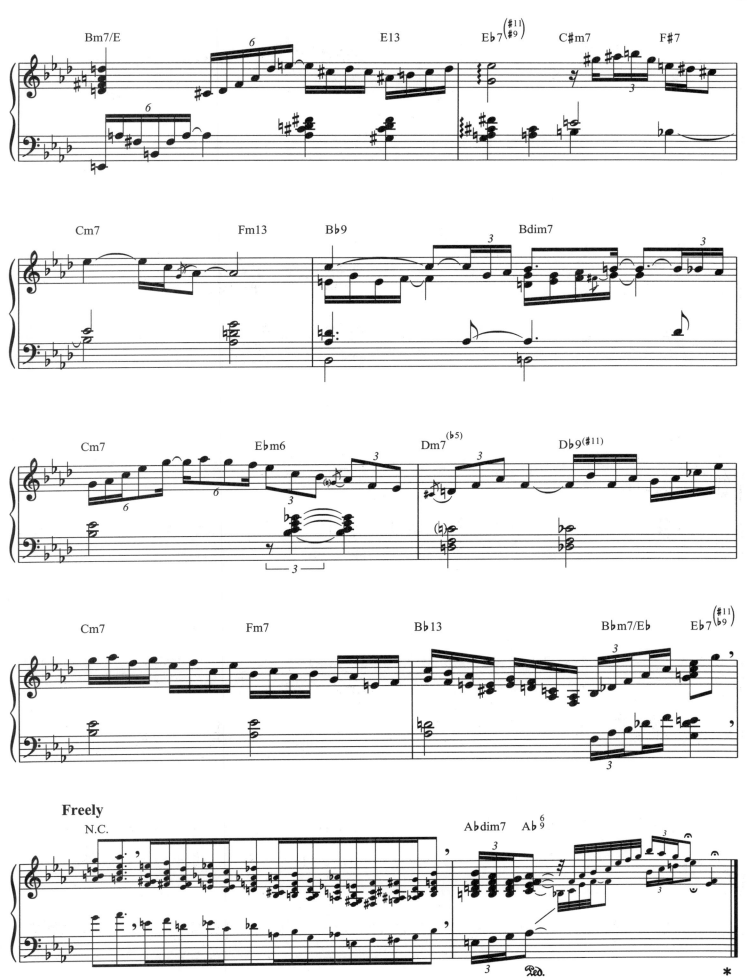

THE TOUCH OF YOUR LIPS

Words and Music by RAY NOBLE

The Touch of Your Lips – 18 – 1

The Touch of Your Lips – 18 – 2

56

The Touch of Your Lips – 18 – 3

58

The Touch of Your Lips – 18 – 5

The Touch of Your Lips – 18 – 6

60

The Touch of Your Lips – 18 – 7

* Transcribed from original recording. Meter changes should be interpreted freely.

The Touch of Your Lips – 18 – 8

The Touch of Your Lips – 18 – 10

The Touch of Your Lips - 18 - 11

The Touch of Your Lips – 18 – 12

The Touch of Your Lips – 18 – 14

68

The Touch of Your Lips – 18 – 15

The Touch of Your Lips – 18 – 16

The Touch of Your Lips – 18 – 18

WHAT IS THIS THING CALLED LOVE

By COLE PORTER

Up tempo (bebop)

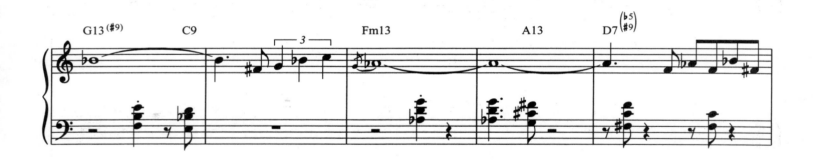

What Is This Thing Called Love – 12 – 1

What Is This Thing Called Love – 12 – 2

74

Piano Solo

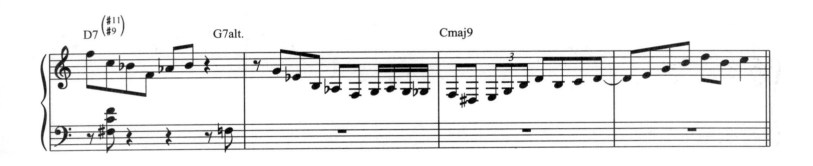

What Is This Thing Called Love – 12 – 4

What Is This Thing Called Love – 12 – 6

What Is This Thing Called Love – 12 – 8

80

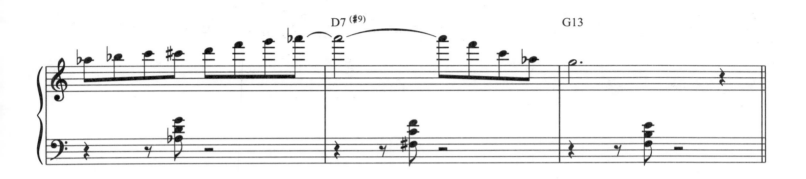

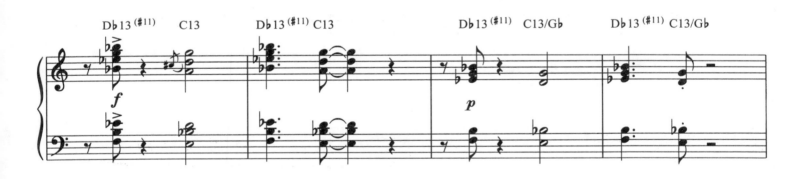

What Is This Thing Called Love – 12 – 12

WHAT KIND OF FOOL AM I

By LESLIE BRICUSSE and ANTHONY NEWLEY

Slowly and freely

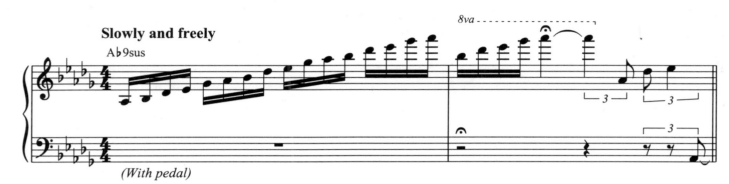

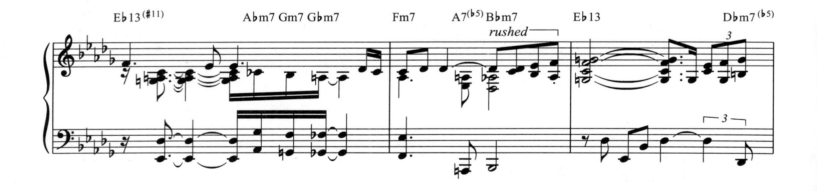

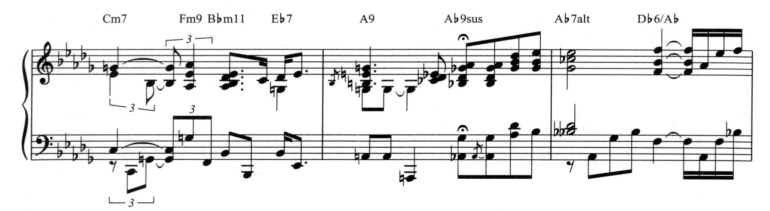

What Kind of Fool Am I – 13 – 1

What Kind of Fool Am I – 13 – 3

What Kind of Fool Am I – 13 – 5

What Kind of Fool Am I – 13 – 6

92

What Kind of Fool Am I – 13 – 9

Tempo I

What Kind of Fool Am I – 13 – 12

96

What Kind of Fool Am I – 13 – 13